THE
SPOOK
BOOK

Also by Burton and Rita Marks

Give a Magic Show!
Kites for Kids

THE SPOOK BOOK

by Burton and
Rita Marks

Illustrated by
Lisa Campbell Ernst

LOTHROP, LEE & SHEPARD BOOKS
NEW YORK

To Alice
for her confidence in us

Text copyright © 1981 by Burton and Rita Marks
Illustrations copyright © 1981 by Lisa Campbell Ernst
Printed in the United States of America. First Edition.
1 2 3 4 5 6 7 8 9 10

Library of Congress Cataloging in Publication Data
Marks, Burton.   The spook book.   Summary: Presents directions for
making a variety of decorations, refreshments, stunts, and games for
Halloween parties.   1. Halloween decorations—Juvenile literature.
2. Handicraft—Juvenile literature.   3. Cookery—Juvenile literature.
[1. Halloween decorations.   2. Parties.   3. Handicraft.   4. Cookery]
I. Marks, Rita.   II. Ernst, Lisa Campbell.   III. Title.
          TT900.H32M37   790.1'922   81-5004
   ISBN 0-688-00425-3   ISBN 0-688-00426-1 (lib. bdg.)   AACR2

Contents

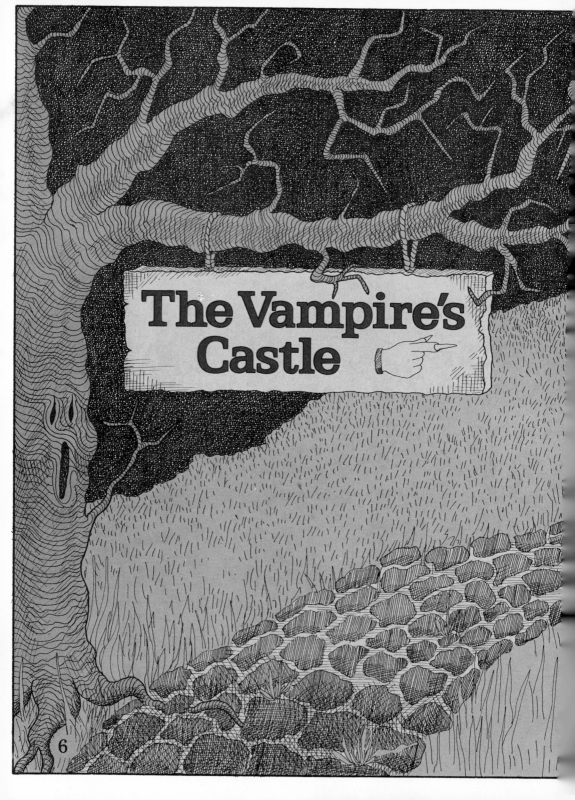

The Vampire's Castle

6

The Vampire's Castle is one of the scariest of all haunted houses. Are you brave enough to walk through it? There is a tour starting on the very next page.

Welcome and Guided Tour

Good evening.
Welcome to our quaint little castle.
It's so nice to have someone drop by.
Here, let me take your coat.

What's inside?
Why, nothing unusual.
It looks like any other castle.
There are a few bats about.
And maybe a ghost or two
... or three.

We do have some other guests.
They're rather strange, but friendly.
I know you'll like them.
Come right in. I'll show you around myself.

Oh, don't bother to close the door.
Someone will do that for you.

We come first to the Witch's Den.
Walk softly here.
The Witch is stirring up a magic brew.
She does not speak or bat an eye...
until a visitor comes near.
Then she screeches her cackly, hollow laugh
and lifts her grisly arms—
to almost *grab* the *passerby*.

Now let's stroll through the graveyard,
where the ghouls and goblins play.
They float above the marble stones
and wail their ghostly moans and groans.

A pleasant place, don't you agree?
Too bad we cannot stay awhile
but there's one more sight we want to see.

13

Our last stop is the Vampire's Tomb.
Shhh, don't make a sound.
The Vampire is mixing secret potions
and does not like to be disturbed.
But wait!
Something is wrong.
The potions are growing larger
and larger and LARGER!

Hey, what's your hurry?
Do not run.
Our night of fun has just begun.

Rat
toenails

Fish
Scales

Dried
Spider
Webs

Frog
Hairs

Building the Castle

You can create the Vampire's Castle in your basement, attic, or any large room. First, mark off a walkway, placing a chair at each corner. Then run a clothesline from chair to chair.

Witch's Den

Enter Here

Next, set up the three Castle scenes on the outside of the walkway. Get your friends to help make the props and costumes. One person can play the Vampire, another the Witch, and a third can greet your guests as they come in.

When everything is ready, cover the windows with dark paper. Then light the room with flashlights to give it a ghostly glow. Stand the flashlights in milk cartons so the lights shine on the ceiling.

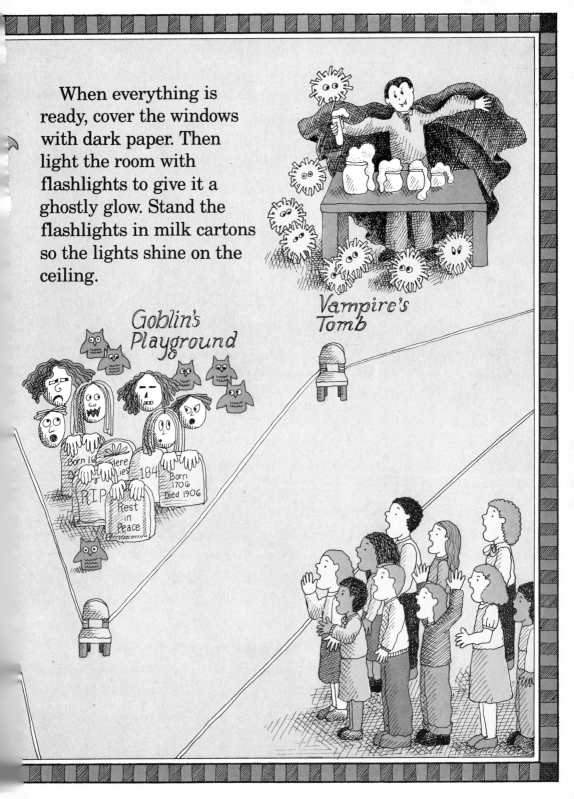

Vampire's Tomb

Goblin's Playground

Sound effects will add just the right touch of terror. Borrow a tape recorder if you can. Or have some friends hidden about the room. Then test your visitors' courage with these.

Moans and Groans— Blow softly over the top of a soft-drink bottle.

Raindrops—Drop rice in a foil pan. Or tap the bottom of the pan with your fingers.

Thunder—Rattle a sheet of lightweight posterboard.

Crackling Fire— Crinkle up a cellophane bag.

Rattling Bones— Shake some nails inside a large tin can.

Heavy Footsteps— Pound your palms, one by one, on the bottom of an empty cardboard carton.

Screeching Owl—Cut a strip of paper about the size of a dollar bill. Make a V-fold in the center as shown. Then cut a small hole in the fold edge. Hold the paper firmly against your mouth with a finger on each side of the V-fold. Then blow HARD!

Before you get too carried away, here are a few tips to remember:

1. Use waterproof felt markers for drawing on balloons, glass, foil, or plastic. Look for the words *waterproof* or *permanent* on the label.
2. Use rubber cement for gluing.
3. Use masking (not cellophane) tape and strong black thread for hanging objects from ceilings and walls.

Making the Props and Costumes

The Witch's Den

Witch's Broom—Cut away the bottom of a large grocery bag. Lay the bag flat and fringe either end almost to the opposite side. Next, roll the uncut edge around one end of a long cardboard tube. Attach with tape. Then tie with heavy string or cord.

tape
and
string

Witch's Cauldron—Use a round plastic clothes basket for the cauldron. Cover the outside with black crepe paper or dark cloth. For stirring the brew, use a broom handle or a heavy stick.

To make the fire, crinkle a large piece of red cellophane and place it under the cauldron. Slip a small flashlight under the cellophane to "light" the fire.

Witch's Costume—For the hat, make a tube of black crepe paper to fit your head. Glue the tube closed and let dry. Then twist one end to a point. Turn up the other end and stretch it outward to form the brim.

For the cape, use a large black plastic trash bag. Tape back one end to form a collar. Pin the collar in the front.

Flying Bats—Trace around the three sides of a wire hanger on black paper. Draw a scalloped

twist

fold up

tape

trash bag

edge along the bottom. Draw the bat's head as shown. Use pieces of orange reflective tape for the eyes. Or cut the eyes from foil gift wrapping and glue in place.

Cut out the bat. Tape it to the hanger. Tie a long thread to the hook and hang up.

The Goblin's Playground

Tombstones—Stuff newspaper into a large grocery bag. Cover the bag with a white plastic can liner. "Engrave" the liner with a black marker. Drape white rubber gloves over the top.

Floating Faces—Blow up a white balloon. Tie the neck with a long thread. Draw a face with a black marker, pressing lightly. For hair, tape on strips of tissue paper or yarn, any eerie color. Hang from the ceiling.

Hoot Owl—Turn a large grocery bag upside down. Cut out wings and ears from the top and sides as shown. Fold forward.

Draw the owl's features and feather markings with bright-colored paint (use fluorescent or Day Glo paints if you have them). Glue foil circles to the center of the eyes. For hanging, tape one end of a long piece of thread to the tip of each ear.

Hanging Webs—Stretch a cord high above the Castle walkway. Tape in place. Then tie on short pieces of black thread so the ends are just above eye level. In the dark they will feel like silky spider webs.

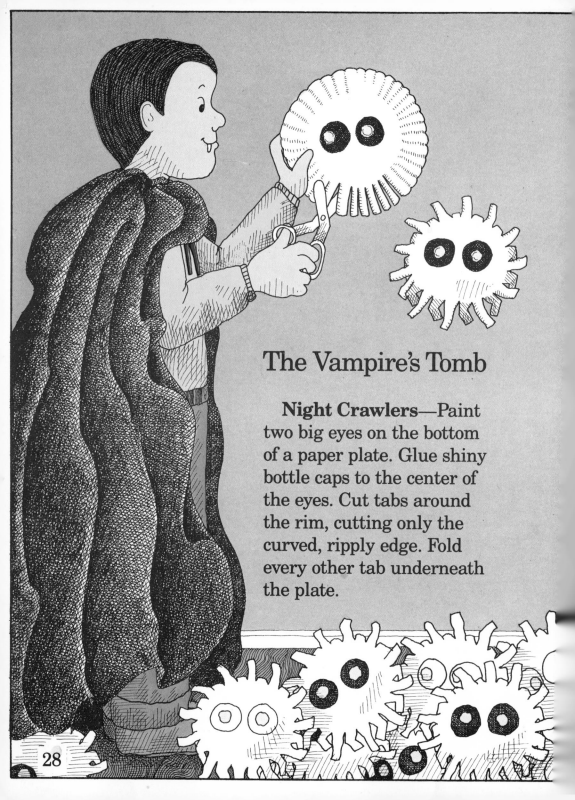

The Vampire's Tomb

Night Crawlers—Paint two big eyes on the bottom of a paper plate. Glue shiny bottle caps to the center of the eyes. Cut tabs around the rim, cutting only the curved, ripply edge. Fold every other tab underneath the plate.

Vampire's Wig—Use a grocery bag that just fits your head. Paint the outside black and let dry. Then fold the bag flat, pressing the bottom halves together. Cut out the wig pattern as shown.

Open the bag and tape the four corners down to make a rounded shape. Cut sideburns from the leftover painted bag and glue them in place.

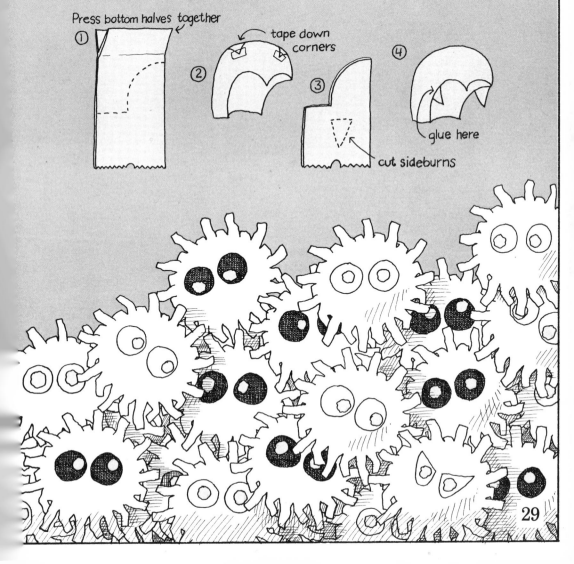

Press bottom halves together

① tape down corners ②

③ cut sideburns

④ glue here

Vampire's Costume—Make a cape from a black plastic bag. (See the witch's cape, page 22.) Slip a red ribbon under the collar before taping it closed. Tie the ribbon around your neck and wear white gloves if you have them.

Fangs—With scissors, cut two long teeth from a marshmallow. Slide one in each corner of your mouth between your upper lip and gum.

Props—Cover a small table with black paper or aluminum foil. Place empty glass jars of different shapes and sizes on the table. To make secret potions, you will need baking soda, soap powder, and vinegar. For the formula, turn to page 52.

Party at the Hall of Horrors

And now, my friend,
we have a special treat for you.
We're giving a little party tonight
and you're invited.

Just step into this secret chamber.
Our other guests are there already.
I'm sure you'll want to meet them—
they're dying to meet you.

Come right ahead.
You'll have a wonderful time.
There will be lots of surprises
and all kinds of good things to eat—
things you can really sink your teeth into.

I know it's rather dark in here.
But our friends seem to like it that way.
Just follow close behind me.
Don't be shy—there's nothing to be afraid of.

Well, almost nothing…

Devilish Decorations

Here are some ideas for changing your party room into a real Hall of Horrors.

Hang a Monster in the Doorway—Cut down the sides of a large green plastic bag. Open the bag and lay it flat. Then cut long narrow slits from one end to make the monster's legs. For eyes, glue on round foil pans. Draw the eyeballs with felt markers or

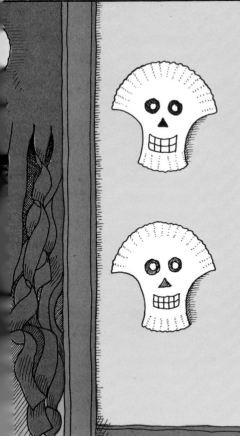

tape bicycle reflectors to the center of the pans.

Tape the monster across the entrance to your party room. Hang a sign in front that says:

DANGER.
GOBLINS AT PLAY.
ENTER AT YOUR OWN RISK!

Helping Hands—Fill white gloves with tissue paper. Tie one to a door knob. Stick another under a closet door or hang from a partly opened drawer.

Scary Skulls—Cut opposite sides of a paper plate as shown. Draw a skull face with a black crayon or marker. Tape the skull to a window or wall, or hang with thread from an open doorway.

Ghostly Lights—Colored lightbulbs will make your party room look very spooky. Green or blue bulbs look best, but any colors will do. If you do not have colored bulbs, use ordinary white ones and color them with felt markers.

Haunting Hang-ups—Hang Floating Faces (see page 25) all about the room.

Spooky Spider—Paint the inside and outside of a small paper cup black. With scissors, fringe the sides of the cup. Bend these "legs" in half as shown. Use two notebook reinforcing rings for the spider's eyes.

Let the spider run loose on the party table or hang from the ceiling with thread.

Spider Web—Cut a piece of plastic wrap the size you want the web to be. Lay it on a sheet of light-colored paper. With a black marker, draw a web. Then peel the plastic from the paper. Stick it on a mirror, a window, or any place you wish.

Plastic Wrap

↖ paper

Marker

Ghoulish Goodies
(that you can conjure up yourself)

Creepy Crawlers

YOU WILL NEED:
20 round snack crackers
whipped cream cheese
thin pretzels

WHAT TO DO:
For each Creepy Crawler:
1. Spread a thin layer of cream cheese on one side of a cracker.
2. Put pretzel "legs" around the edge.
3. Spread cream cheese on a second cracker and place on top of the pretzels.
4. Store in the refrigerator until serving time.

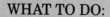

Makes 10 crawlers

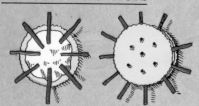

A Sweet Variation

Use vanilla or chocolate wafers instead of crackers. For the filling, use ready-made vanilla pudding or frosting. Or use jelly instead of cream cheese in step three of the cracker recipe.

Zombies

YOU WILL NEED:
10 slices of bread
peanut butter
raisins, bananas, figs,
nuts, puffed rice

WHAT TO DO:
1. Toast the bread
   lightly. Then spread
   one side with peanut
   butter.
2. Now make a spooky
   face for each guest.
   Use banana slices and
   raisins for eyes. A
   walnut half or fig can
   be a nose. Form the
   mouth with raisins or
   peanuts. Use almonds
   or puffed rice for teeth.

Makes 10 zombies

39

Phantom Floats

This purple potion is terrible to look at. But it tastes delicious!

YOU WILL NEED:
1 quart grape juice
1 quart ginger ale
1 quart lime sherbet
whipped topping

WHAT TO DO:
For each serving:
1. Half-fill a glass with grape juice.
2. Add a scoop of lime sherbet.
3. Add ginger ale until the glass is almost full. Stir.
4. Spoon on a glob of whipped topping.

Makes about 8 chilling floats

Warning: Have more of everything on hand. Phantom Floats disappear quickly!

Give Your Friends the Willies

With a black marker, draw a creepy creature on the *outside* bottom of each glass. Then watch your guests squirm when they discover something "crawling" in their floats.

To remove the creatures, wash off with soap and water.

Coconut Uglies

YOU WILL NEED:
1 quart chocolate ice cream
peanuts
unsweetened flaked coconut
black or red licorice strings

WHAT TO DO:
For each Coconut Ugly:
1. Scoop a ball of ice cream onto a sheet of wax paper.
2. Sprinkle with coconut "hair." Press on peanuts for eyes. Cut licorice strings into short pieces for the tails and antennae.
3. Store in the freezer until serving time.

Makes about 10-12 uglies

Vampire's Punch

YOU WILL NEED:
1 quart cranberry juice
1 quart orange juice
½ cup raspberry sherbet, softened
Vampire's Eyes Cubes

WHAT TO DO:
1. Mix the juices together.
2. Add the sherbet and stir until it disappears.
3. Before serving, chill with the Vampire's Eyes Cubes.

Makes 10-12 servings

Vampire's Eyes Cubes

YOU WILL NEED:
grape juice or cranberry juice
seedless green grapes
large muffin tin

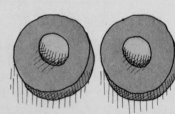

WHAT TO DO:
1. Half-fill the muffin cups with juice. Freeze until slushy (about ½ hour).
2. Push a grape into the center of each cup. Refreeze until solid.

Tip: To remove the cubes, float the tin in warm water.

Popcorn Ghosts

YOU WILL NEED:

10 cups popped popcorn

25 marshmallows

1 tablespoon margarine or butter

dark raisins

WHAT TO DO:

1. Put the marshmallows and margarine in a 3-quart saucepan.
2. Place the pan on the stove with the heat turned very low. Ask someone older to help you with this.
3. Stir the mixture with a wooden spoon until the marshmallows are melted (about 10 minutes).
4. Remove the pan from the stove and pour the mixture over the popcorn in a large bowl.
5. Stir until the popcorn is coated with marshmallow.
6. Pour the popcorn onto wax paper to cool (about 3 or 4 minutes).
7. Grease your hands lightly with margarine or butter. Divide the popcorn into 10 parts. Form each into a ball-shaped head with a long nose. Press on raisins for the eyes and mouth.

Makes 10 ghosts

Eerie Entertainment

This evening would not be complete without
games and stunts and magic tricks.
Our friends have promised a chilling show.
So sit back and enjoy it.
But just one thing—
please try not to faint.
It spoils *all* the fun.

Spooky Stunts
and Gruesome Games
Tell-a-Tale

The best way to start off a spook party is with
a story—a *very scary* story. For the scariest
story ever, just set the scene. Then ask your
friends to add to the terrible tale. You might
begin this way:

I will never forget that winter night when I took
a shortcut home from a party after school. It was
cold and the wind was blowing. The streetlights
had just come on and long shadows were creeping
across my path. I knew I had to hurry to be home
before dark.

Suddenly I heard a strange noise just ahead.
Then something snapped behind me, again and
again. I stopped and looked around. I was in front
of an old house I couldn't remember seeing before.
Its porch was sagging and the windows were
covered with dust. It seemed to be empty except
for a flickering light in an upstairs room.

Now the wailing ahead was getting louder and the snapping sounds behind were coming closer and closer. I decided to make a run for the old house. I opened the gate and crossed the overgrown yard. Huge trees blocked the fading daylight and I could barely see where I was going. I felt my way along the basement wall. Then all of a sudden the wall gave way and I fell onto something soft. I looked up and found myself *inside* the house.

Now you stop and point to a friend to tell the next "chapter." Keep the story going until everyone has had a turn.

Ghost Watching

Draw a ghost on black paper. Cut it out, cutting holes for the eyes and mouth, too. Then paste it to a sheet of white paper.

Now stare at the ghost while you count slowly to thirty-five. Then look at a light-colored wall. In a few seconds a ghost will appear there—a white ghost. And as you watch, it will slowly float across the room.

Stare at the ghost until it disappears. Then blink your eyes hard. The ghost will return. But just long enough to wave goodbye.

Ask the Spirits

You don't believe in spirits? Try this!

Take a piece of string and tie a ring to one end. Hold the other end in either hand with the tips of your fingers. Then ask the spirits a question that can be answered yes or no. They will answer through the ring. If the answer is yes, the ring will move back and forth. If the answer is no, it will move in a circle.

How does it work? Nobody knows for sure. But the spirits answer every time.

Mystery Messages

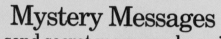

You can send secret messages by using a white candle and a plain sheet of white paper. Write your message with the end of the candle. No one will be able to see what you have written—not even you.

Now chant these words in an eerie voice:
Spirits, spirits, write for me
a message that we all can see.

Then take a pencil and color the sheet of paper. Slowly, just like magic, your message will appear.

Sleepy Ghost

Here's how to wake up a sleeping ghost. On white paper, draw a ghost about the size of your hand. Cut it out. Then fold along the dotted lines shown, bending the arms first, then the head.

Put some water in a shallow dish. (This is the ghost's water bed.) Float the ghost in the water and say, "Wake up, spook. It's time to rise." Slowly the ghost will lift his head. Then he will open his arms.

Try the same trick with other cutouts, too.

51

The Vampire's Potion

Here's a special formula for young spooks and vampires.

Put two large spoonfuls of baking soda and a spoonful of soap powder in a tall glass jar. Next, half-fill a cup with vinegar and pour it into the jar.

Instantly the potion will bubble and foam. Then it will creep up to the top of the jar and slowly ooze out over the sides.

Place a large dish under the jar to catch the spills.

The Ghoul's Remains

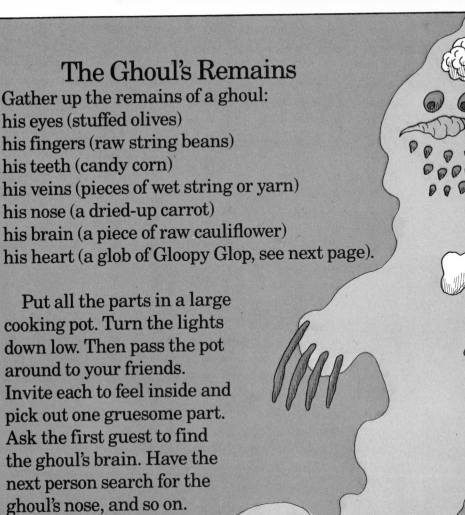

Gather up the remains of a ghoul:
his eyes (stuffed olives)
his fingers (raw string beans)
his teeth (candy corn)
his veins (pieces of wet string or yarn)
his nose (a dried-up carrot)
his brain (a piece of raw cauliflower)
his heart (a glob of Gloopy Glop, see next page).

Put all the parts in a large cooking pot. Turn the lights down low. Then pass the pot around to your friends. Invite each to feel inside and pick out one gruesome part. Ask the first guest to find the ghoul's brain. Have the next person search for the ghoul's nose, and so on.

As soon as the pot is empty, turn up the lights so everyone can see what they've *really* found.

A Farewell Gift
Gloopy Glop

Make Gloopy Glop for the Ghoul's Remains on the previous page. It's also a perfect take-home gift for guests at a Vampire's Castle.

What can you do with Gloopy Glop?

You can squeeze it, squish it, roll it, stretch it, mold it. You can tear it into a million pieces, then stick the pieces together again. Slowly... slowly... Gloopy Glop will melt back into one big rubbery glob.

YOU WILL NEED:

½ cup liquid laundry starch

½ cup white liquid school glue (such as Elmer's)

WHAT TO DO:

1. Pour the starch and glue into a small plastic bowl.
2. Mix them together with your hands until you have one big gooey piece (about 5 seconds). Don't worry if your hands get sticky—Gloopy Glop washes off with soap and water.

Tip: Store Gloopy Glop in the refrigerator to keep it soft and spongy.

"Good night, my friend."